First published in Belgium and Holland by Clavis Uitgeverij, Hasselt – Amsterdam, 2010
Copyright © 2010, Clavis Uitgeverij

English translation from the Dutch by Clavis Publishing Inc. New York
Copyright © 2017 for the English language edition: Clavis Publishing Inc. New York

Visit us on the web at www.clavisbooks.com

Race Car Drivers and What They Do written and illustrated by Liesbet Slegers
Original title: *De autocoureur*
Translated from the Dutch by Clavis Publishing

ISBN 978-1-60537-321-8

This book was printed in February 2017 at Publikum d.o.o., Slavka Rodica 6, Belgrade, Serbia

First Edition
10 9 8 7 6 5 4 3 2 1

Clavis Publishing supports the First Amendment and celebrates the right to read

Race Car Drivers
and What They Do
Liesbet Slegers

Clavis

NEW YORK

Auto racing is a very exciting sport.

The most famous auto races are called Formula One.

Formula One races take place all over the world.

Only the very best drivers can participate.

It's fun to watch these races on TV.

Who will cross the finish line first?

helmet (with a small tube for drinking, a radio and a microphone)

The race car driver's suit should be fireproof – even his underwear!

The driver also wears a special helmet: there is a sort of straw inside,

so that he can drink while driving.

He has to keep his hands on the wheel, of course.

There is also a microphone in the helmet

so he can talk with his team during the race.

The helmet protects his ears from the loud noise of the race car.

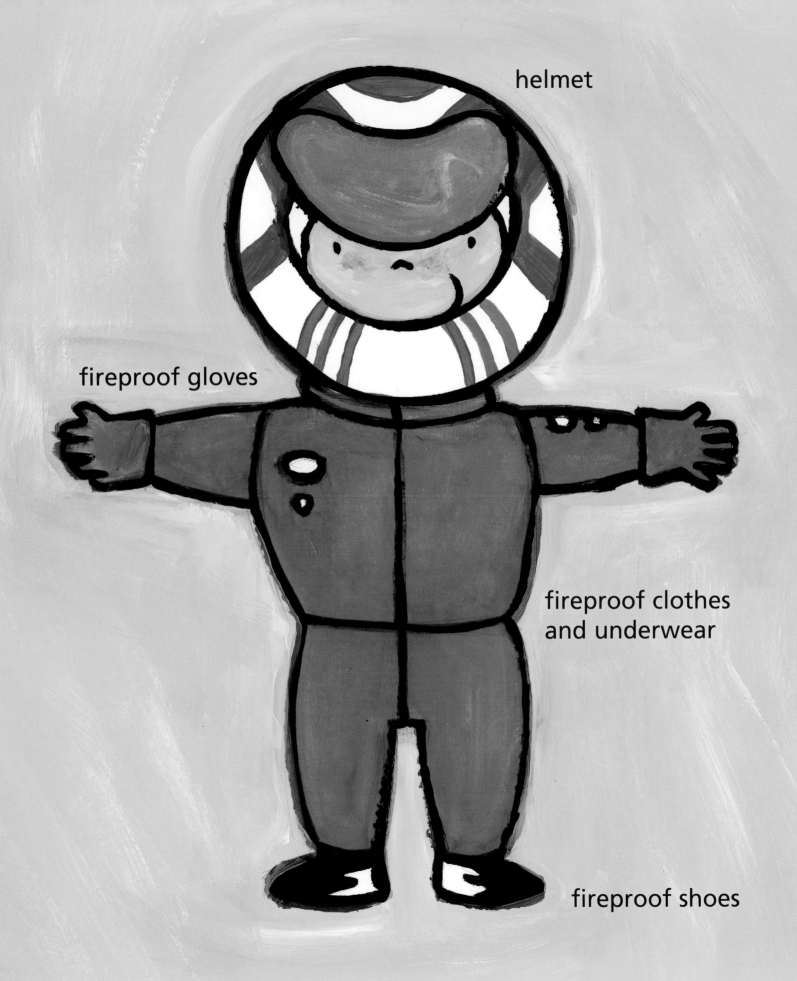

helmet

fireproof gloves

fireproof clothes
and underwear

fireproof shoes

A race car driver can only win a race

if his super-fast racing car is in perfect shape.

Race car drivers drive along a circuit: a big loop with many turns.

The driver belongs to a team with other drivers and car mechanics.

Car mechanics work in a pit: a small workplace along the circuit.

During the race, the racing car stops in the pit

to get new tires or more gas. This happens extremely fast.

The car can also be repaired very quickly.

race car

circuit

pit

car mechanics

A race car driver should be strong and healthy,
because driving at top speed is hard work!
That's why a race car driver practices a lot
and eats plenty of vegetables and fruit.
It's not easy to become a race car driver.
First you have to go to a real driving school!
You can become a Formula One driver only if you are
very good at driving.

A Formula One driver has to prepare for every competition.

On the first day, he will study the circuit.

A bend to the left, then a straight section,

then two bends to the right....

The driver often explores the circuit on foot or by bike!

Meanwhile the race car is transported in a big truck.

That truck also contains extra tires and other equipment,

such as tools to tune the motor.

The second day is a time trial: one by one, the drivers try to complete
one tour of the circuit as fast as possible. This is important, as
the fastest drivers can start in front position in the real competition.
There isn't enough room for all the cars in the first row.
Well, by now the racing driver has prepared himself enough.
He knows the circuit by heart and is ready for the big day.

The third day is the big day: the actual race.

All engines are running loudly. It is a deafening sound.

The driver sits nervously at the wheel with his helmet on his head and his seat belt firmly fastened.

When the red light goes out, all the cars shoot ahead.

Within seconds they are driving at top speed!

During the race it gets very warm inside the driver's suit.

It's a good thing he can drink water through the small tube

in his helmet. A bend to the left, then a straight section,

then two bends to the right. Luckily, he has memorized the circuit.

Everyone drives as fast as he can.

It's getting extremely exciting!

Because they are going at top speed,

the car's tires get quickly worn out.

That's why the racing driver stops at the pit.

He talks through the radio to the team that's waiting in the pit.

Things should go quickly, or else his car will fall behind.

The other drivers won't wait!

In a few seconds the four tires have been changed and…

WHOOSH, the car hits the road again!

The race car driver has to pay attention to the flags along the circuit.

A yellow flag means danger – for instance, in case of an accident.

A green flag means that the danger is over.

A blue flags warns that a driver wants to overtake another driver.

And at the finish line, they wave a black-and-white checkered flag.

Then we know who the winner is.

The winner gets a big trophy on the podium.

The first three to cross the finish line are overjoyed.

They shout and jump because they are happy with their results.

The cork pops and champagne spurts out of the bottle.

Let the party begin!

Toy cars are fun, but being a real Formula One driver is really great!
You can already start training.
Who knows? Someday you might also become a speed champion.
As a runner, a cyclist or… a race car driver!